Science Alive!

Weather

CRABTREE
Publishing Company
www.crabtreebooks.com

How to use this book

Each chapter begins with experiments, followed by the explanation of the scientific concepts used in the experiments. Each experiment is graded according to its difficulty level. A level 4 or 5 means adult assistance is advised. Difficult words are in boldface and explained in the glossary on page 32.

Crabtree Publishing
www.crabtreebooks.com

PMB 16A, 350 Fifth Avenue,
Suite 3308, New York
New York 10118

612 Welland Avenue,
St. Catharines, Ontario
Canada L2M 5V6

**Published in 2003
by Crabtree Publishing Company**

Published with Times Editions
Copyright © 2003 by Times Media Private Limited

Series originated and designed by
TIMES EDITIONS
An imprint of Times Media Private Limited
A member of the Times Publishing Group

Coordinating Editor: Ellen Rodger
Project Editors: P. A. Finlay, Carrie Gleason
Production Coordinator: Rosie Gowsell
Series Writers: Darlene Lauw, Lim Cheng Puay
Series Editor: Oh Hwee Yen
Title Editor: Katharine Brown
Series Designers: Rosie Francis, Lynn Chin
Series Picture Researcher: Susan Jane Manuel

Cataloging-in-Publication Data
Lauw, Darlene.
    Weather / Darlene Lauw and Lim Cheng Puay.
        p. cm. — (Science alive!)
    Includes index.
    Summary: Introduces concepts related to weather through various activities and projects.
    ISBN 0-7787-0565-X (RLB) — ISBN 0-7787-0611-7 (PB)
    1. Meteorology—Juvenile literature. 2. Weather—Juvenile literature.
3. Weather—Experiments—Juvenile literature.   [1. Weather.
2. Weather—Experiments. 3. Experiments.]   I. Lim, Cheng Puay. II. Title.
III. Series: Lauw, Darlene. Science alive!
    QC863.5.L38 2003
    551.5—dc21
                                                                2002011641
                                                                        LC

Picture Credits
Marc Crabtree: cover; Art Directors & Trip Photo Library: 1, 6, 7 (middle and right), 14 (bottom), 22 (right), 23, 26 (bottom and middle); Bes Stock: 14 (top); Corel: 31; Danish Tourist Board: 15; Digital Stock: 18, 19, 30; HBL Network Photo Agency: 10; North Wind Picture Archives: 11; Topham Picturepoint: 22 (left), 27

Printed and bound in Malaysia
1 2 3 4 5 6—0S—07 06 05 04 03 02

INTRODUCTION

Weather is what we see and feel outdoors. It rains and storms on some days, and the sun shines on others. The movement of air causes weather to change but what causes clouds and rain? Where does wind come from? How is lightning produced? Find out more about weather by reading and doing the science experiments in this book!

Contents

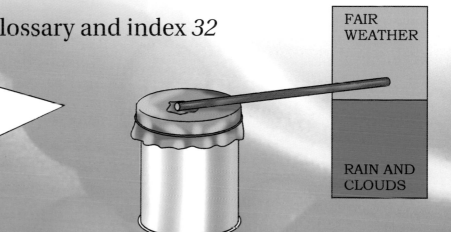

The power of the sun!

Surrounding Earth are layers of **gases** called the atmosphere. The closest layer to Earth, which is the troposphere, is where all our weather occurs. When the sun shines, the land and water on Earth absorb heat. Air passing over Earth is heated, which causes our weather to change. The higher away from Earth, the colder the air is.

Before clocks were invented, people used the position of the sun to tell the time. They did this by using a sundial, or shadow clock.

Difficult — 5
4
Moderate — 3
2
Easy — 1

You will need:
- A glass jar
- A piece of cardboard
- A pencil
- Scissors
- A ruler
- Glue
- A knitting needle
- Plasticine
- Tape
- Three pieces of wood
- A world atlas

Make your own sundial

1 Place the mouth of the jar on the piece of cardboard. Using the pencil, trace the outline of the jar's mouth. Cut the outline with the scissors. The cutout makes a lid for the jar.

2 Cut a strip of cardboard measuring the **circumference** of the jar. You can do this by wrapping a strip of cardboard around the jar and cutting off the overlapping edges.

3 Use the ruler and pencil to divide the cardboard strip into 24 equal sections. Number these sections from one through 24. Then divide each section into four.

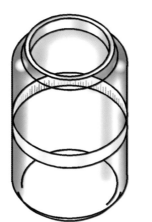

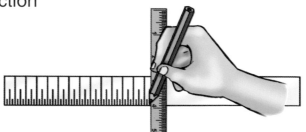

4 Glue the cardboard strip halfway up inside the jar as shown in the diagram. Make sure that the markings are facing inward.

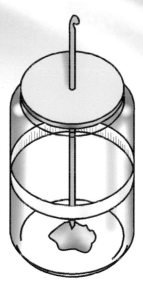

5 Push the knitting needle through the lid of the jar. Then use the Plasticine to fix the point of the knitting needle on the base of the jar. Secure the lid to the jar with tape.

6 Make a stand for the jar like the one shown in the diagram. The tilt of the stand should equal 90 degrees minus your latitude. Your latitude is the distance north or south of the equator. Use an atlas to estimate the latitude of your location. After you have calculated and measured your latitude, glue the wood pieces into place.

7 Position the jar and its stand so that it faces the sun when it is noon, or one o'clock during Daylight Saving Time (DST). Turn the jar until the needle's shadow falls exactly on the "12" mark. Then glue the jar to the stand.

8 Your sundial now shows "sun time." The knitting needle casts a shadow to indicate the hour of the day or the quarters of the hour. Remember that your sundial is a 24-hour clock so, after noon, you will need to subtract twelve from the hour to calculate the time.

The sun as a clock!

In the *Make Your Own Sundial* experiment, you saw that Earth receives different amounts of sunlight at different times of the day. This is because Earth is tilted on an **axis** and rotates, or turns, 360 degrees every 24 hours. Dividing Earth into the northern and southern hemispheres, or halves, is an imaginary line known as the equator. The equator runs around the middle of Earth. Areas of the world that lie closest to the equator are called the tropics and receive more of the sun's heat than areas away from the equator, near the North and South Poles. The movement of air around Earth cools some areas and heats others. If air did not move around our planet, we would not have weather. Air movement is also necessary to prevent extreme hot or extreme cold temperatures. Without moving air, some areas would be too hot for anything to survive and other areas would be completely frozen over with ice.

The sun is almost directly overhead at the equator. Places located near the equator, such as Tobago (*left*), have very hot weather because the sun's rays hit the ground straight on.

The history of sundials

Throughout history, people have measured time by studying the movement of the sun and stars. The earliest sundial dates back to 3500 B.C. and was called an obelisk (*right*). The obelisk was a tall, four-sided pillar built by the ancient Egyptians. People could tell time by looking at the obelisk's shadow.

Another type of sundial was the hemispherical sundial (*below*) first described by the **astronomer** Berossus in the third century B.C. This sundial was more advanced than the obelisk, because it allowed for changes in time according to the different seasons.

Did you know?

There are some months in the year when the sun does not set at the North and South Poles. This is because Earth is tilted. As Earth moves around the sun, different parts are closer to the sun, resulting in the changing of seasons. When the North Pole tilts toward the sun, it is summer in the northern hemisphere and winter in the southern hemisphere. The South Pole receives almost no sunlight while the North Pole has constant sunlight for six months. This period at the North Pole is referred to as the time of the "midnight sun."

SAVING TIME!

Daylight Saving Time (DST) lets people make use of the longer hours of daylight during summer. Daylight Saving Time also saves energy because we use less electricity for lighting and appliances when we have more hours of sunlight. DST starts at 2 a.m. on the first Sunday of April in most parts of North America. On this day, clocks are put forward one hour. DST ends at 2 a.m. on the last Sunday of October when clocks are put back one hour.

The weight of air affects weather!

A thick layer of gases called the atmosphere extends from Earth into space. The weight of all these gases builds up the closer you are to Earth. The farther away from Earth you are, the less weight there is pressing down on you. This weight is known as air pressure.

A barometer is a device that measures air pressure. Try making your own barometer!

■ Ask an adult for help

Difficult — 5
          4
Moderate — 3
          2
Easy —   1

You will need:
• Scissors
• A balloon
• A tin can
• An elastic band
• Glue
• A straw
• Cardboard
• A ruler
• A pen
• Tape

Making a barometer

1 Cut the balloon so that it opens up. Stretch it across the top of the tin can and secure it in place using the elastic band.

2 Glue one end of the straw to the center of the balloon so that the straw rests horizontally on the balloon.

3 Make a weather chart. Cut a piece of cardboard twice the height of the can and 2 inches (5 cm) wide. Using the ruler, draw a line through the halfway point of the cardboard. Write "fair weather" on the top half of the cardboard and "rain and clouds" on the bottom half. Tape your weather chart on a wall and place your barometer next to it. Make sure the straw touches the chart.

4 When the air pressure outside the can is greater than the pressure inside the can, the weight of the air on the can presses the surface of the balloon down. The straw then tilts upward, indicating fair weather. The straw will point to the bottom half of the chart when it rains or is cloudy.

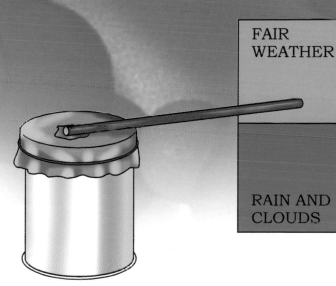

FAIR WEATHER

RAIN AND CLOUDS

A water barometer!

Difficult — 5
4
Moderate — 3
2
Easy — 1

You will need:
- One teaspoon of food coloring
- A glass of water
- An empty soda bottle
- A marker

1 Add the food coloring to the glass of water.

2 Choose a soda bottle that has a cylinder larger than the mouth of the glass. Flip the bottle upside down into the glass. Make sure that the mouth of the bottle does not touch the bottom of the glass.

3 If no water enters the bottle, tip the bottle a little to allow some water to enter the neck of the bottle.

5 Check the bottle every day to see if the water level changes.

4 Using the marker, draw a line on the glass to indicate the water level within the bottle.

Air pressure and the weather

The air's pressure changes with the weather. Higher air pressure outside the can made the straw in the *Making a Barometer* experiment point up to indicate fair weather. In the experiment *A Water Barometer*, higher air pressure pushing down on the water in the cup forced more water into the bottle. Air pressure is the weight of the atmosphere pressing down on Earth. The amount of pressure depends on the amount of air above the point of measurement. Warm weather means greater air pressure, while **precipitation** means low air pressure.

      Temperature, or the hotness or coldness of the air, also affects air pressure. Warm air rises, then cools before it sinks back to Earth. Air is made up of **molecules**. When air is warmed by the land or water it passes over, the molecules start to move farther apart, making the air lighter, so it rises. Likewise, when air is cooled, the molecules move closer together, and the cooler air sinks. When warm air is closer to Earth, the air pressure is low and the air will rise to form clouds and rain. High pressure means the weather will be clear, because cool air is sinking toward Earth.

At **sea level** there is more air pressing down on Earth so there is higher air pressure. At the top of a mountain, there is low air pressure, because there is less air above the peak.

What is a barometer?

A barometer is an instrument used to measure air pressure. Evangelista Torricelli (1608–1647), an Italian **physicist** and mathematician, invented the barometer in 1643. He filled a tube with mercury, which is a silvery liquid that is heavier than water, turned it upside down, and plunged it into a bowl also filled with mercury. Some of the mercury from the tube flowed into the bowl, but there was still some mercury left in the tube. Torricelli concluded that the weight of air, or air pressure, on the mercury in the bowl, prevented all of the mercury in the tube from emptying out. The mercury moved higher up the tube as air pressure increased. If the air pressure decreased, the mercury went down in the tube. The air pressure changed according to changes in weather.

Did you know?

Marsh gases, such as methane and sulfur, have a "rotten-egg" smell, caused by lack of oxygen in mud. If the air around a marsh or swamp seems to smell more than usual, you can guess that the air pressure is low and it will soon rain. This is because on days of high air pressure, there is enough weight to keep the marsh gases close to the mud. When there is low air pressure, the gases rise into the air more freely because there is less weight on the marsh gases.

POP! POP! POP!

Have your ears ever "popped" as you drove up a mountain or went up in an airplane? This is because you are moving from an area of high air pressure to an area of lower air pressure. Air that is trapped inside your ears rushes out to try to balance the pressure, causing your ears to "pop."

Windy days are fun!

Air moving across the surface of Earth is called wind. Meteorologists, or scientists who study the weather, observe wind speed and direction to predict changes in the weather using weather vanes and **anemometers**.

■ Ask an adult for help

Difficult — 5
— 4
Moderate — 3
— 2
Easy — 1

You will need:
- A pencil
- A ruler
- Three pieces of cardboard, two rectangular pieces measuring 4 X 12 inches (10 X 30.5 cm) and one square piece measuring 7 X 7 inches (18 X 18 cm)
- A pocketknife
- Tape
- Two paper clips
- Scissors
- Plasticine
- A marker
- Two heavy rocks

A weather vane

1 Using the pencil and ruler, divide one of the rectangular pieces of cardboard into five sections as shown. Ask an adult to run the pocketknife along the lines as shown. Do not cut through the cardboard.

2 Make a base by folding the cardboard along the five sections. Make a hole in the middle with the point of the pencil. Then push the pencil through the hole. Use the tape to attach the folded cardboard base to the square piece of cardboard. This is the stand for your weather vane.

3 Straighten out the two paper clips. Wrap one paper clip loosely around the blunt end of the pencil and the other one loosely around the tip of the pencil as shown in the diagram. Then take the paper clips off the pencil.

4 Draw an arrow, like the one shown, on the other rectangular piece of cardboard. Cut out the arrow shape.

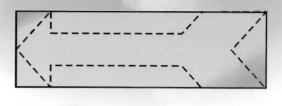

5 Use the Plasticine to attach the pencil to the center of the arrow. Make sure that you use an equal amount of Plasticine on both sides of the pencil to balance the arrow properly.

6 Use the tape to attach one paper clip under the hole in the stand and the other paper clip to the base directly underneath. Now stand the pencil in the hole.

7 Mark the points of the **compass** on the base: "N" for North, "E" for East, "S" for South, and "W" for West. Put your weather vane outdoors. Point the base of your weather vane so that "E" faces the direction of the rising sun in the east. You may need to use the two heavy rocks on either end of the base to hold your weather vane in place.

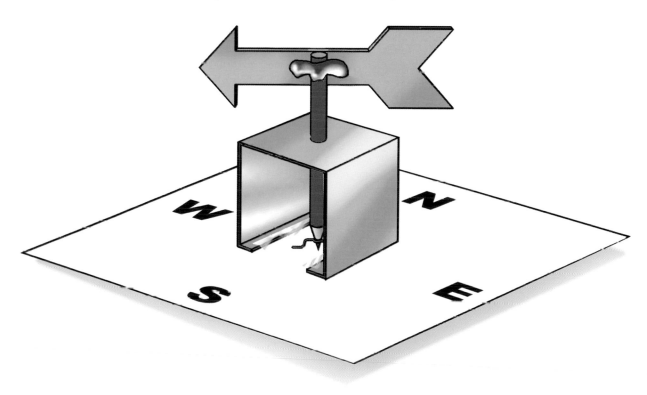

What makes wind blow?

As warm air (low pressure) rises, cooler air (high pressure) rushes in to take its place. This rushing air is what we feel as wind. The high-pressure air passing over the surface of Earth results in what is known as surface wind. The greater the difference between the low pressure and high pressure, the stronger the wind.

Winds are named by the direction from which they blow. The arrow on a weather vane (*right*) points toward the direction from which the wind is blowing. So, if the vane points toward "N," it means that the air is moving from the north.

There are different types of wind. Strong winds, such as this tropical typhoon, sometimes form over warm waters but die down over land.

Windy instruments

While a weather vane shows which direction the wind is blowing from, an anemometer measures wind speed. Anemometers consist of three or four cups that are attached to a rotating pole which stands 30 feet (nine meters) above the ground. The wind fills the cups and makes them turn. The cups rotate faster when the wind is stronger. To calculate wind speed, meteorologists count the number of rotations the cups make in a given length of time.

Wind turbines, which are like modern windmills, convert wind energy into electricity. The blades on a turbine either face the wind or face away from the wind. The wind turns the blades, which spin a shaft, or a long bar. This shaft is connected to a generator that makes electricity. For a large wind turbine to make electricity for your house, the wind has to blow pretty hard — about 18 miles per hour (29 km per hour).

Did you know?

Jet streams are bands of fast-moving air that move at speeds of up to 150 miles per hour (241 km per hour) at heights of about six miles (ten kilometers) above the ground. Jet streams form when warm and cold air meet. These streams usually move from west to east.

WIND POWER!

Wind can be used to produce **electricity**, a form of **energy**. In regions that have strong winds, windmills transform wind energy into power for our homes and industries. Power generators in the windmills convert the energy of moving wind into electrical energy. Wind energy is environmentally friendly because it is pollution-free. It will also never run out!

Water, water everywhere!

More than two-thirds of Earth's surface is covered with water. Water is also present in Earth's atmosphere. Water exists as a gas in water vapor, a liquid in water, and a solid in ice. Water on Earth moves in a continuous cycle, called the water cycle. Water travels from Earth's surface, rises into the atmosphere, and then falls back to Earth's surface as precipitation.

You will need:
- A tin can
- Ice cubes
- A piece of wood
- A bowl of warm water

Rain making

 1 Fill the tin can with ice cubes.

 2 Place the piece of wood over the bowl of warm water.

3 Put the tin can on the piece of wood. What do you see forming on the outside of the can?

Water vapor in the atmosphere **condenses** to form millions of tiny water droplets when the air cools. These water droplets then join together to form clouds. When the water droplets get too heavy to stay in the clouds, the droplets fall as rain. This next experiment shows you how to make your own clouds.

Difficult — 5
— 4
Moderate — 3
— 2
Easy — 1

You will need:
- A cup of cold water
- A large clear-glass bottle with a tight-fitting cork
- A teaspoon of talcum powder
- A piece of paper, folded in half
- A corkscrew

Making clouds!

 Pour the cold water into the bottle and seal it with the cork.

2 Remove the cork after a few minutes. Place the talcum powder on the paper. Using the paper, quickly pour in the talcum powder and then replace the cork.

3 Push the cork farther into the neck of the bottle, using the corkscrew as a handle.

4 After about thirty seconds, pull the cork out a little. Watch what happens!

How do clouds and rain form?

In the *Making Clouds* experiment, pressing the cork farther into the neck of the bottle increased air pressure in the bottle. This happened because you were squeezing the air and packing the air molecules into a smaller space. The energy you exerted caused the air inside the bottle to get warmer. This heat evaporated some water in the bottle and water vapor formed. As you pulled the cork out, the air pressure in the bottle dropped, and the air cooled. Some of the water vapor then condensed into water droplets. These water droplets clung to the talcum powder, forming a small cloud.

Rain is formed by condensation. In the *Rain Making* experiment, the water vapor in the air around the can cooled and condensed into water droplets you saw on the outside of the can. In clouds, these droplets join together to form larger drops, which eventually become too heavy to remain in the clouds. These droplets fall from the clouds as rain.

Almost all of the water that **evaporates** from the oceans, seas, and lakes falls back into them through the water cycle. The rest falls mostly on the land, soaks into the soil, and seeps into rocks. This water eventually finds its way back to the ocean, sea, a river, or a waterfall (*page 19*).

Continuous rain that lasts for hours or even days occurs in a type of cloud called a nimbostratus cloud. A nimbostratus cloud is a low, gray and usually dark cloud that produces rain or snow. Its base is located between 1,970 and 8,202 feet (600 and 2,500 m) above the ground.

Running water!

The water cycle is a never-ending process. The sun's rays heat the land, oceans, seas, and lakes. Near the ground where air pressure is high and the air is warm, water evaporates to form water vapor. As it rises, the air expands and cools. The water vapor in the air then condenses on tiny **particles** of smoke and dust that are in the air to form clouds. Water droplets from clouds fall back to Earth as rain or, if it is cold enough, as snow or hail. Most of this water falls back into Earth's seas, oceans, lakes, or rivers. The sun's heat evaporates the water and the water cycle begins again.

Did you know?

Scientists have learned how to make rain through a process called cloud seeding. To make rain, an airplane carrying small pieces of materials, such as dry ice, or carbon dioxide in solid form is flown through clouds. The particles are released into the clouds. Water vapor clings to these particles. The water droplets then become heavy enough to fall as rain.

RAINING ICE

What causes hail to form instead of rain? **Convection currents** in a storm cloud carry water droplets upward, away from the warm surface of Earth. As the droplets move higher in the cloud, they cool. When the temperature of the droplets falls below freezing point, the water freezes. The convection currents then carry the frozen water droplets down to the bottom of the cloud. This cycle occurs many times, and the frozen water droplets become bigger and bigger each time. When the droplets are too heavy to stay in the cloud, they fall as hail.

Light rain, heavy rain

Raindrops are between 0.08 and 0.2 inches (2 and 5 mm) wide. Large raindrops splash when they hit the ground, while smaller raindrops fall to Earth as drizzle. Meteorologists use rain gauges to measure rainfall. You can make your own rain gauge.

■ Ask an adult for help

Difficult — 5
— 4
Moderate — 3
— 2
Easy — 1

Measuring rain

1 Make a scale to measure the rain. Use the ruler and pencil to mark intervals from 0 to 3 inches (0 to 8 cm) on the strip of paper.

2 Tape the scale vertically to the outside of the bottle as shown in the diagram. Put tape over the whole scale so it is completely waterproof.

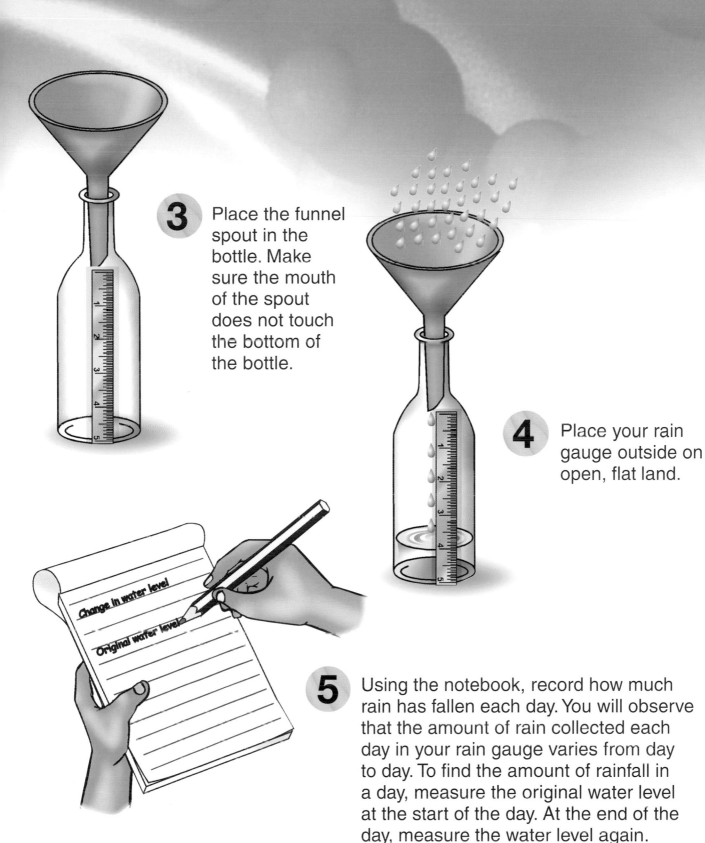

3 Place the funnel spout in the bottle. Make sure the mouth of the spout does not touch the bottom of the bottle.

4 Place your rain gauge outside on open, flat land.

Change in water level

Original water level

5 Using the notebook, record how much rain has fallen each day. You will observe that the amount of rain collected each day in your rain gauge varies from day to day. To find the amount of rainfall in a day, measure the original water level at the start of the day. At the end of the day, measure the water level again. Subtract your final measurement from the original water level. This is the change in water level, or the amount of rainfall your rain guage collected in that day.

21

The powers of the rain gauge

Rainfall measurements tell you how much water falls on a particular place during a period of time. Farmers use rain gauges to measure how much rain falls on their land, so they can decide if they need to find other sources of water for their crops. Modern rain gauges are very advanced. They accurately measure amounts of rainfall to one-hundredth of an inch (0.3 mm). Some rain gauges are even designed to melt frozen precipitation such as snow, sleet, and hail that fall into the funnel. Changing frozen precipitation into water allows scientists to measure and record precipitation more accurately.

Summer monsoons, or winds, in Asia blow in over the land from the sea. These winds collect moisture as they move across the sea. Then the winds release the moisture over land as heavy rain.

Rainfall is measured by recording how much water collects in a rain gauge (*above*). The rain gauge is placed on flat, level ground in an open space. The rainwater falls into the funnel and runs down into a measuring cylinder.

Who invented the rain gauge?

The son of the Korean king Sejong invented the first rain gauge in 1441. King Sejong ordered the inhabitants of each village in the kingdom to measure and record rainfall levels regularly. He believed this would help them predict the wet and dry months.

The villagers dug holes in the earth and measured how much rain fell into each hole. The different sizes and shapes of the holes made the readings inaccurate. King Sejong's son solved this problem by giving each villager an identical metal container with a funnel on the rim and a scale on the side. This device was the first rain gauge.

Q QUIZTIME

Name the world's wettest town.

Answer: Cherrapunji in northwest India. Between August 1860 and July 1861, Cherrapunji received a record high of 1,042 inches (2,646 cm) of rain. Each year, Cherrapunji receives about 394 inches (1,000 cm) of rain. It rains so much in Cherrapunji because it is located 4,232 feet (1,290 m) above sea level. Warm air over the plains and valleys cools as it rises to Cherrapunji, forming clouds and then rain.

Did you know?

You may have heard of the expression "raining cats and dogs," but have you heard of "raining toads"? In June 1997, it rained toads in the town of Villa Angel Flores, Mexico! A small **tornado** whirled up a cluster of toads from a pond and dropped them all over the town in the Pacific coastal state of Sinaloa.

RAIN, RAIN, GO AWAY!

People do not always welcome rain. When it rains heavily for days, floods (*below*) can occur. Flooding usually happens because it rains too much in a short period of time. Dams, rivers, and lakes cannot contain all of the water, so it overflows and floods the land. Flooding also occurs when the rain comes after a long dry period and the ground is too hard to soak up the rain. Rainwater builds up on the ground's surface and flooding occurs. Floods destroy crops and put human lives at risk. Landslides can also be the result of too much rainfall. Landslides happen when rock or soil soak up rainwater and slide down mountain sides.

What a muggy day!

Humidity is the amount of moisture in the air. When water evaporates to form water vapor, the air carries the water vapor with it. On days of high humidity there is a lot of water vapor in the air. On days of low humidity there is little water vapor in the air, so the air is dry. Try these experiments to see how you can measure humidity and use it to predict the weather.

Difficult — 5
— 4
Moderate — 3
2
Easy — 1

You will need:
- Glue
- A dry pinecone
- Two sheets of cardboard
- Tape
- A straw
- A marker pen

Pinecone weather

1 Glue the base of the pinecone to a sheet of cardboard.

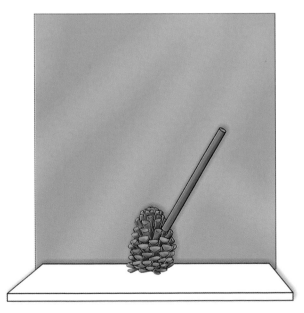

2 Tape the straw to one of the pinecone's scales, about halfway up the pinecone.

3 Place the pinecone next to a wall in a sheltered area outdoors. Stick the other sheet of cardboard on the wall, behind the pinecone. Make sure that the straw touches the cardboard.

4 Using the marker pen, mark the point where the straw touches the cardboard. Leave the pinecone.

 5 Note the position of the straw the next time you see a storm brewing. Mark the new position on the cardboard. Do you see that the straw moves to a position directly above the pinecone?

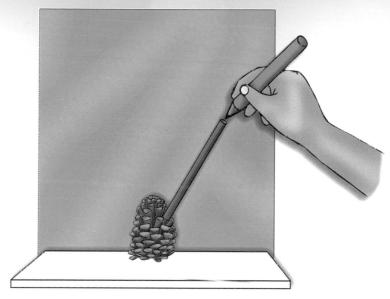

Measuring air moisture

 1 Tape the two thermometers side by side onto the wall.

Difficult — 5
— 4
Moderate — 3
— 2
Easy — 1

You will need:
- Tape
- Two thermometers
- A wall
- A piece of cotton cloth
- A cup of water
- A pencil or pen
- A notebook

 2 Wrap the cotton cloth around the bulb of one thermometer, leaving a trailing end. Tie it in place securely. Dip the end of the cloth into the cup of water so that the cloth soaks up water.

3 Compare the temperature readings of the two thermometers from time to time. Record the thermometer readings. What do they tell you? The greater the temperature differences between the two readings, the lower the level of air moisture.

25

What is humidity?

Humidity is the amount of moisture in the air. The moisture is in the form of water vapor. When air absorbs as much water vapor as it can, the air becomes saturated, or completely soaked with moisture. Warm air can hold more water vapor than cold air because the molecules in warm air are spread farther apart, leaving more space for water vapor. In cold air, water vapor condenses to form water droplets.

The pinecone in the experiment *Pinecone Weather* measured how wet the air was. In the heart of a pinecone are its seeds. Pinecones release their seeds on warm, dry days. On cold, wet days, pinecones close up to protect their seeds from the damp, moving the straw as a result.

Heat is lost as water evaporates to form water vapor. Did you notice that the wet bulb of the thermometer in the experiment *Measuring Air Moisture* cooled more on dry days than on humid days? The difference in readings between the two thermometers is small on a humid day and greater on a dry day.

As warm, moist air cools to the point of saturation, the water vapor condenses into water droplets. This saturation point is known as the dew point. Fog occurs when warm, moist air flows over much colder ground. The warm, moist air is cooled from below as it flows over a colder surface. If the air is near saturation, it condenses into fog.

Measuring humidity

A hygrometer, such as this one, is a device that measures the amount of humidity in the air. Scientists have invented many kinds of hygrometers. The dry-and-wet-bulb psychrometer is one type. You made this hygrometer in the experiment *Measuring Air Moisture*. We can compare readings from a thermometer wrapped in cotton cloth and another thermometer exposed to air to measure humidity levels.

There is even a hygrometer that uses human hair to determine humidity. This type of hygrometer is called a mechanical hygrometer. Human hair stretches when it absorbs moisture. Hair expands when humidity rises and contracts when humidity decreases. As the hair length changes, it moves a needle attached to a scale. These readings can then be used to estimate the amount of moisture in the air.

QUIZTIME

In which area will air have higher humidity?
a) An area close to the ground or ocean
b) An area high up in the mountains

Answer: a. Air that is close to the ground is warmer and, therefore, can absorb more water vapor. This water vapor comes from the evaporation of oceans, rivers, and lakes.

Did you know?
Humidity can be used to forecast the weather. A stuffy, humid day indicates that it will probably rain. If air humidity is low, the air feels dry, signaling a dry spell.

HARMFUL HUMIDITY

Some farmers do not harvest grain crops when the weather is humid. Moist air can cause **mold** to grow on the grains while they are in storage. Farmers can only harvest such crops when the weather is dry.

Flash, crash, boom!

Thunderstorms occur when warm air is forced quickly upward in the atmosphere, and the warm and cool air collide. During a thunderstorm, bright flashes of lightning light up the sky and you hear thunder. What is lightning? How is thunder made? Let's find out!

You will need:
- A rubber glove
- Plasticine
- A large baking tray
- A large plastic bag
- A table
- A tin can

Creating a spark!

1 Put on the rubber glove. Use your other hand to press the Plasticine firmly onto the baking tray.

2 Spread the plastic bag out on the table and place the tray on it.

3 Holding the bag still, grasp the Plasticine and move the tray around vigorously.

4 After thirty seconds, pick up the tray by the Plasticine, using one hand. Using your gloved hand, hold the tin can so that the shiny base of the can is close to the corner of the tray. See what happens. A spark will jump from the tray to the can!

28

Lightning and thunder happen at the same time. So why do we see lightning before we hear thunder? Light travels at a speed of 186,420 miles per second (300,000 km per second), while sound travels at a speed of 1.9 miles per second (3 km per second). This means that lightning travels much faster than thunder. In the previous experiment, you made lightning. Now try to make thunder!

Difficult — 5
— 4
Moderate — 3
— 2
Easy — 1

You will need:
• A paper bag
• A pen with a sharp ball point

Paper bag thunder!

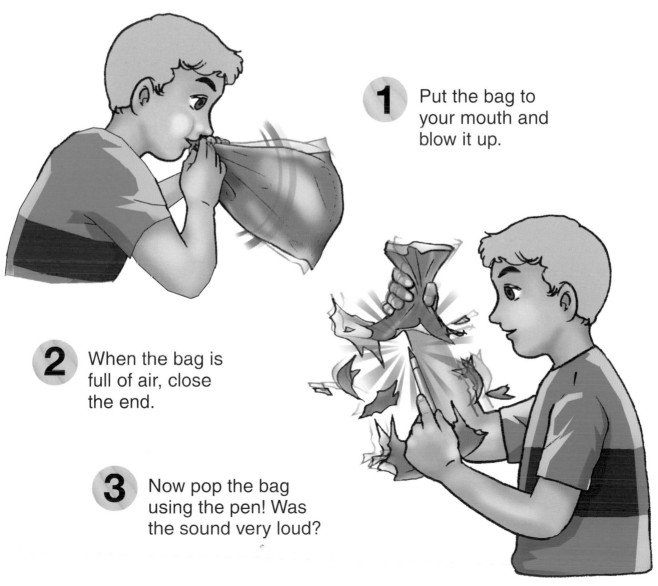

1 Put the bag to your mouth and blow it up.

2 When the bag is full of air, close the end.

3 Now pop the bag using the pen! Was the sound very loud?

Lightning and thunder

Thunderstorms occur in cumulonimbus clouds. These clouds are tall, stretching for miles into the atmosphere. Inside the cloud, warm air carrying water vapor travels to the top of the cloud, cools, and freezes into ice crystals. In the *Creating a Spark* experiment, the movement of the tray resembles the way water droplets and ice crystals move inside the cloud. As these particles move against one another, the particles become charged. When you placed the tin can beside the tray in the experiment, the charged particles in the tray were attracted to the particles in the can, creating a small amount of electricity that you saw as a spark.

Thunder accompanies lightning. Lightning produces a lot of heat, with temperatures reaching 54,000°F (29,982°C)! These extremely high temperatures cause the surrounding air to expand very quickly. This air expansion creates large **sound waves**. These sound waves push through the air until they reached your ears, and you hear thunder. In the experiment *Paper Bag Thunder,* popping the bag released a rush of outgoing air. The air carried the sound to your ears.

When **atoms** bump against one another, they lose or gain **electrons**. The loss of electrons results in positive charges, and the gaining of electrons results in negative charges. Opposite charges attract, and like charges repel. In a cloud, positive charges gather at the top of the cloud, and the negative charges gather at the bottom. The negative charges in the cloud are attracted to positive charges on the ground or in a neighboring cloud. This results in the flash of electricity known as lightning.

Lightning detection

Over the years, scientists have learned a lot about lightning. Today, scientists use lightning as a tool to study the size and movement of thunderstorms. Meteorologists in the United States detect and track thunderstorms and lightning using the National Lightning Detection Network (NLDN). A system of magnetic **sensors** and computers form this network throughout the country. When lightning strikes the ground, sensors detect the electrical charge of lightning. These sensors then locate almost immediately where the strike took place.

Did you know?

About 44,000 thunderstorms occur every day worldwide and produce 100 lightning flashes per second. In the United States alone, about 25 to 30 million lightning bolts hit the ground each year. The state of Florida is known as the lightning capital of the United States. Each year, the central part of the state, where it is warmest, experiences about 90 thunderstorm days and almost twice the number of lightning strikes as in other parts of the country. In contrast, lightning rarely strikes areas in the North or South Poles because these regions lack the heat that produces thunderstorms.

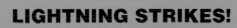

LIGHTNING STRIKES!

Lightning can strike as far as 25 miles (40 km) away from the main storm, so it can be dangerous to go outside shortly after the rain has stopped. If you can hear thunder, the storm is probably close enough for lightning to strike. You should remain in a building or vehicle until you cannot hear thunder anymore.

Glossary

anemometer (page 12): An instrument that measures the speed of wind.

astronomer (page 7): A scientist who studies objects beyond Earth's atmosphere.

atom (page 30): The smallest unit of matter. Inside an atom are neutrons, protons, and electrons.

axis (page 6): The imaginary line extending through Earth from the North Pole to the South Pole.

circumference (page 4): The outer boundary of a circular area.

compass (page 13): A device used to determine location and direction.

condense (page 17): To change a gas or vapor into a liquid or solid form.

convection currents (page 19): The circular movement of a gas or liquid when heated.

electricity (page 15): A form of energy that generates light and heat.

electron (page 30): A particle in an atom that has a negative charge.

energy (page 15): Power used to do work.

evaporation (page 18): The change from a liquid or solid state into gas.

gas (page 4): The form of a substance that is neither liquid or solid. Gases expand freely to fill a space. Air is a gas.

mold (page 27): A type of fungus, or fuzzy growth, that forms on a damp object.

molecules (page 10): The smallest unit of matter, made up of one atom or more.

physicist (page 11): A scientist who specializes in the study of physics.

precipitation (page 10): Water that falls to Earth as rain, snow, sleet, or hail.

sea level (page 10): The level of the surface of the ocean, used as a standard in measuring land elevation or sea depth.

sensor (page 31): An instrument that reacts to particular conditions, such as heat or light, and then sends a signal to a measuring or control device.

sound waves (page 30): Energy in the form of waves caused by a vibrating object. The waves reach our ears as sound.

tornado (page 23): A violent, whirling column of air.

Index